DECONSTRUCTING POWERFUL SPEECHES

FREDERICK DOUGLASS

WHAT TO THE SLAVE IS THE 4TH OF JULY?

REBECCA SJONGER

A Crabtree Classics Book

Crabtree Publishing

crabtreebooks.com

Author:
Rebecca Sjonger
Series research and development:
Janine Deschenes and Ellen Rodger
Editorial director:
Kathy Middleton
Editor:
Ellen Rodger
Proofreader:
Roseann Biederman
Graphic design:
Katherine Berti
Image Kantor:
Rebecca Sjonger and Katherine Kantor
Print coordinator:
Katherine Kantor

Images:
Alamy, North Wind Picture Archives: p. 17
BlackPast.org: p. 33 (bottom right)
Flickr, Boston Public Library: p. 10 (top)
Getty Images, Michael Zagaris: p. 40–41
Gilder Lehrman Institute of American History: p. 7 (bottom right)
INK—ODW Newspaper Collection: p. 35 (bottom)
Internet Archive
Boston Public Library, Gleason's pictorial drawing-room companion: p. 8 (bottom), 11 (bottom left)
Open Library: p. 12 (top)
The Liberator Files: p. 33 (center left)
Library of Congress: p. 3, 7 (center), 11 (top right), 22, 38
Detroit Publishing Company: p. 43 (bottom)
Kurz & Allison: p. 26–27
Lindsley, Harvey B.: p. 23 (top)
Serial and Government Publications Division: p. 19, 33 (bottom left)
National Park Service: p. 6 (bottom left)
Shutterstock, Everett Historical: p. 25
University of Michigan, Life and Times of Frederick Douglass: p. 5 (bottom right)
Wikimedia Commons
Bettman:Corbis, through The New York Times photo archive, photographer William H. Cheney, South Orange, NJ: p. 23 (bottom)
Boston Public Library: p. 6 (bottom right)
Clark Art Institute, Gilbert Stuart: p. 24 (bottom right)
Cliff, Flickr: p. 7 (top left)
The Daguerreian Society, Chester County Historical Society: p. 34 (bottom left)
Delaware Art Museum, Howard Pyle: p. 21
Edinburgh Emancipation Society in 1866: p. 20
Eduardo Montes-Bradley: p. 42
Engraved by J.C. Buttre from a daguerretotype: p. 4 (top)
Frank Fey (U.S. Senate Photographic Studio), Office of Senator Ted Cruz: p. 40 (bottom right)
Google Cultural Institute, John Trumbull: p. 24 (center right)
Internet Archive Book Images: p. 8 (center right)
John Lewis Krimmel: p. 30
Joostvandeputte: p. 33 (center right)
Joseph Duplessis: p. 24 (center left)
Library of Congress: p. 34 (top right), 36–37
Historic American Buildings Survey: p. 5 (top)
Restoration by Adam Cuerden: p. 9 (top)
Maps Etc—Florida Center for Instructional Technology at University of South Florida: p. 28–29
Missouri History Museum: p. 32
National Gallery of Art, Washington, Gilbert Stuart: p. 24 (center far left), 24 (center far right)
National Archives, Goerge Kendall Warren: p. 11 (top left)
National Archives of Canada: p. 35 (top)
Rosetta Douglass Sprague: p. 6 (top left)
Smallcurio from Austin, TX: p. 5 (bottom left)
The Johnson Collection: p. 28 (bottom)
US National Park Service: p. 28 (bottom left), 39
White House
John Vanderlyn: P. 24 (bottom center)
Rembrandt Peale: p. 24 (bottom left)
William C Teller: p. 43 (top)
www.loc.gov—Screen Shot 2020-04-22 at 2.06.18 PM: p. 13 (bottom)
All other images by Shutterstock

Library and Archives Canada Cataloguing in Publication

Title: Frederick Douglass : What to the slave is the 4th of July? / Rebecca Sjonger.
Names: Sjonger, Rebecca, author.
Series: Sjonger, Rebecca. Deconstructing powerful speeches.
Description: Series statement: Deconstructing powerful speeches | Includes bibliographical references and index.
Identifiers: Canadiana (print) 2020028990X | Canadiana (ebook) 20200289942 | ISBN 9780778781639 (softcover) | ISBN 9780778781592 (hardcover) | ISBN 9781427125897 (HTML)
Subjects: LCSH: Douglass, Frederick, 1818-1895—Oratory—Juvenile literature. | LCSH: Slavery—United States—Juvenile literature. | LCSH: Antislavery movements—United States—Juvenile literature. | LCSH: Speeches, addresses, etc., American—History and criticism—Juvenile literature. | LCSH: Oratory—United States—Juvenile literature.
Classification: LCC E449 .S56 2021 | DDC j973.7/114—dc23

Library of Congress Cataloging-in-Publication Data

Names: Sjonger, Rebecca, author.
Title: Frederick Douglass : What to the Slave is the 4th of July? / Rebecca Sjonger.
Description: New York : Crabtree Publishing Company, 2021. | Series: Deconstructing powerful speeches | Includes bibliographical references and index.
Identifiers: LCCN 2020031631 (print) | LCCN 2020031632 (ebook) | ISBN 9780778781592 (hardcover) | ISBN 9780778781639 (paperback) | ISBN 9781427125897 (ebook)
Subjects: LCSH: Douglass, Frederick, 1818-1895--Juvenile literature. | Douglass, Frederick, 1818-1895. Frederick Douglass Fourth of July oration at Rochester, New York, July 5, 1852. | African Americans--History--Juvenile literature. | Slavery--United States--History--Juvenile literature. | Antislavery movements--United States--History--Juvenile literature. | Speeches, addresses, etc., American--African American authors--Juvenile literature. | African American abolitionists--Juvenile literature. | African American orators--Juvenile literature.
Classification: LCC E449.D75 S56 2021 (print) | LCC E449.D75 (ebook) | DDC 973.8092--dc23
LC record available at https://lccn.loc.gov/2020031631
LC ebook record available at https://lccn.loc.gov/2020031632

Crabtree Publishing

crabtreebooks.com 800-387-7650
 In Canada: We acknowledge the financial support of the Government of Canada through the Canada Book Fund for our publishing activities.

Printed in Canada/032024/CPC20240307

Published in Canada
Crabtree Publishing
616 Welland Avenue
St. Catharines, Ontario
L2M 5V6

Published in the United States
Crabtree Publishing
347 Fifth Avenue
Suite 1402-145
New York, NY 10016

Hardcover 978-0-7787-8159-2
Paperback 978-0-7787-8163-9
Ebook (pdf) 978-1-4271-2589-7

CONTENTS

INTRODUCTION

Frederick Augustus Washington Bailey later took the name Frederick Douglass.

Sophia Auld had no idea what she set in motion when she taught Frederick the alphabet. The bright boy had recently joined the Aulds in Baltimore.

His full name was Frederick Augustus Washington Bailey and he was born in Talbot County, Chesapeake Bay, eastern shore of Maryland. Frederick, like many enslaved children, was taken from his mother, Harriet Bailey, as a baby. He did not know who his father was, although some said he could be Aaron Anthony, the man who owned his mother.

Eastern shore of Chesapeake Bay

The Wye House plantation in Maryland was a stepping stone for young Frederick. He was brought to live there in 1824 at the age of six. In 1826, he moved to Fells Point in Baltimore.

Frederick was eight years old when he was given to the Aulds. Sophia had never owned an enslaved person before. She treated him kindly at first. But she stopped educating him when her husband, Hugh, found out about it. In most southern states it was against the law to teach enslaved people to read or write. Hugh knew that the more Frederick learned, the more difficult it would be to control him.

Frederick was an eager student, however, and he did everything he could to learn more. For help with reading, he traded his daily bread to white children in the neighborhood. He used a piece of chalk to write on fence boards and pavement. Around the age of 13, he got a copy of *The Columbian Orator*. This book included a **debate** in which an enslaved person convinced his owner to set him free. It inspired Frederick. It gave him some hope for a better future.

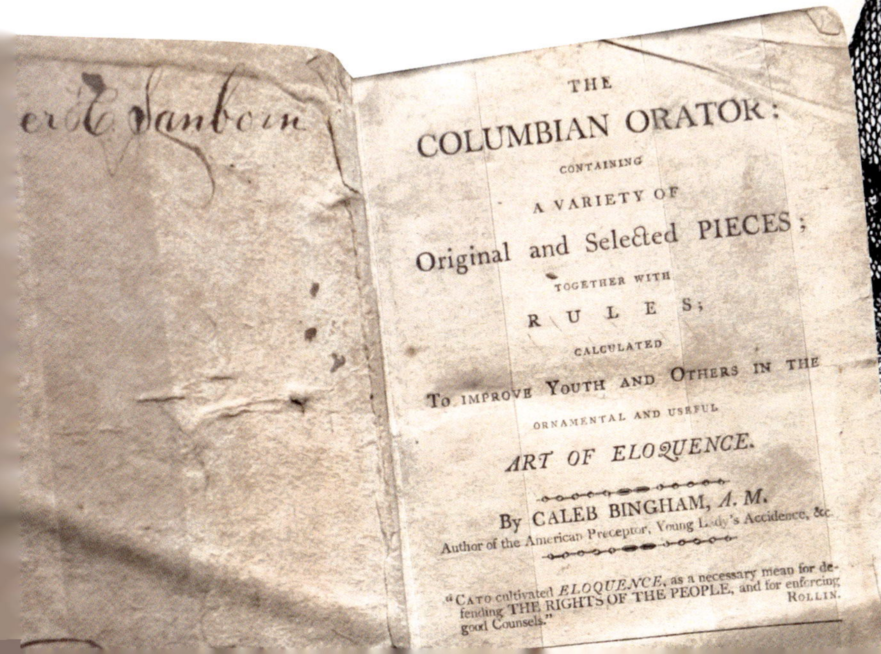

THE COLUMBIAN ORATOR:

CONTAINING

A VARIETY OF

Original and Selected PIECES;

TOGETHER WITH

RULES;

CALCULATED

TO IMPROVE YOUTH AND OTHERS IN THE ORNAMENTAL AND USEFUL

ART OF ELOQUENCE.

By CALEB BINGHAM, A. M.

Author of the American Preceptor, Young Lady's Accidence, &c.

"CATO cultivated ELOQUENCE, as a necessary mean for defending THE RIGHTS OF THE PEOPLE, and for enforcing good Counsels." ROLLIN.

In his narrative of his life, Frederick Douglass describes Sophia Auld as kind at first. But owning humans transformed her and she became cruel.

AN ACTIVIST IS BORN

*Anna (Murray) Douglass was also an **abolitionist**. She and Frederick were married for 44 years.*

Over the years, Frederick was passed from owner to owner. He kept learning whenever he could. He also taught other enslaved people. His goal was always to find freedom, and on September 3, 1838, he reached that goal when he ran away from Baltimore. A free Black woman named Anna Murray helped him escape. The couple married soon after and changed their family's name to Douglass.

Frederick and Anna moved to New Bedford, Massachusetts. He began to speak publicly about his experiences as an enslaved person. The Massachusetts Anti-Slavery Society hired him to help build support for their cause. Douglass spoke so well that some people suspected he had never been enslaved.

Frederick's and Anna's house in New Bedford, Massachusetts

For three decades before the Emancipation Proclamation in the United States, people of African ancestry celebrated the anniversary of the Abolition of Slavery Bill, which was passed across the British Commonwealth, every August 1st.

William Lloyd Garrison was the publisher of an anti-slavery journal called The Liberator. He helped get Douglass's book published.

In 1845, he wrote *Narrative of the Life of Frederick Douglass* to spread the facts. It sold 5,000 copies in the first four months. Despite this success, he was not safe from slave catchers who hunted down runaways and returned them to their owners.

With his book popular, Douglass left America to speak in the United Kingdom. He could travel in safety there as slavery had been abolished in the U.K. in 1833–34. Douglass the author and orator grew friendly with other abolitionists—or people who worked to end slavery. A group of them offered to buy his freedom. This allowed him to return to the U.S. and continue his mission to end slavery in his home country.

Narrative of the Life of Frederick Douglass *is Douglass's first autobiography and his best known one. He published three versions during his lifetime.*

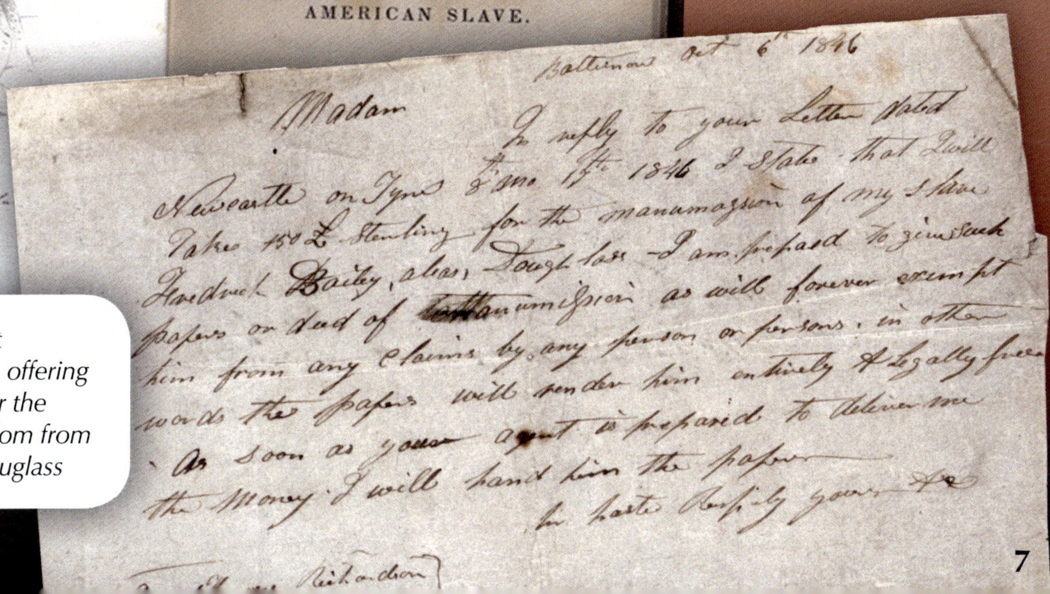

Baltimore Oct 6th 1846

Madam

In reply to your Letter dated Newcastle on Tyne 8 mo 17th 1846 I State that I will Take 150 £ Sterling for the manumission of my Slave Frederick Bailey, alias Douglass — I am prepared to give such papers or deed of manumission as will forever exempt him from any claims by any person or persons. in other words the papers will render him entirely & Legally free. As soon as your agent is prepared to deliver me the Money I will hand him the papers

In haste Respectfully yours &c

A copy of the letter that abolitionist friends sent, offering "150 pounds sterling for the manumission," or freedom from slavery, of Frederick Douglass

INDEPENDENCE DAY SPEECH

The Douglass family settled in Rochester, New York. It was there that Frederick Douglass gave his most well-known speech. The Rochester Ladies' Anti-Slavery Society hosted it at the Corinthian Hall. More than 500 people packed into the grand new building. The mainly white audience paid 12 cents each to hear Douglass. He was described as being forthright and aware of "his dignity and power." At over six feet tall, Douglass's physical presence drew everyone's attention. He stood very straight as he began to speak.

Douglass was familiar with the hall and many of the people there. However, he confessed that he was not at ease. It was Monday, July 5, 1852—the day after Independence Day. It marked America's freedom from Britain 76 years earlier. However, Douglass did not see it as a happy national holiday. He described it as a "sham" instead. He would declare, "I hear the mournful wail of millions whose chains…[are made] more intolerable by" the celebration.

READ IT

This speech is about 10,000 words long. The most accurate full text is printed in books about Frederick Douglass. They can be found in libraries. Sources like this book and most websites use excerpts. These are shorter parts that highlight the main features. For example, check out: **https://to.pbs.org/2Kb5dCE**

Susan B. Anthony, later famous for her work in women's suffrage, began her work as an activist for abolition. Her home became a meeting place for abolitionists.

The Corinthian Hall was an impressive building. It hosted many great speeches over the years.

The northern and southern states disagreed on slavery. This led to a civil war breaking out in 1861.

Douglass questioned the idea of freedom in a country where over three million humans were enslaved. His speech became known as "What to the Slave Is the Fourth of July?" It was a plea for freedom for all people. It came to be one of the most famous anti-slavery **arguments** in history. His message soon spread beyond Rochester. When the **American Civil War** began less than a decade later, Douglass was already a leader among abolitionists. He continues to inspire **social justice** movements today.

TIMELINE

1818	Likely year Frederick Douglass was born
1838	Douglass escaped slavery
1841	Douglass delivered one of his first anti-slavery speeches
1850	*Fugitive Slave Act* allowed escaped enslaved people to be captured across the U.S.
1857	U.S. Supreme Court ruled that African Americans were not citizens
1861–1865	American Civil War
1865	13th Amendment abolishes slavery in the U.S.
1895	Douglass died

CHAPTER 1

PERSUASIVE PRIMARY SOURCES

"What to the Slave Is the Fourth of July?" is a primary source. This firsthand account and others like it bring us as close as we can get to being at a time or event in history. Frederick Douglass's speech revealed some of the struggles enslaved people faced in the mid-1800s. Original images are another example of primary sources. Douglass was the most photographed person in the United States in his **era**. There are even more portraits of him than there are of Abraham Lincoln. Douglass used these photos to present himself to the public. They helped raise his profile as an abolitionist leader.

This book and other secondary sources interpret primary sources. Looking at primary and secondary sources gives a reader a clearer picture of an event.

AN IN-DEPTH LOOK

Secondary sources rely on information found in primary sources. Articles that describe Douglass's speeches and reviews of his books are examples of secondary sources. They interpret, or explain, the original material. These related sources are often created sometime later. They analyze, or study, an issue or event in a variety of ways. Other secondary sources share opinions. Including multiple primary and secondary sources helps give a more in-depth view of the subject matter.

Secondary source

SOURCE ANALYSIS 101

Finding the following facts is the first step in analyzing a primary source. These details help show if the source is useful.

Maker, such as a writer

***Intended** audience*

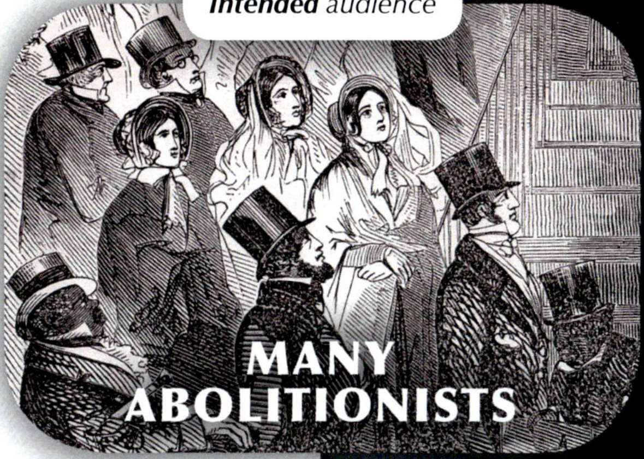

Date delivered

Purpose

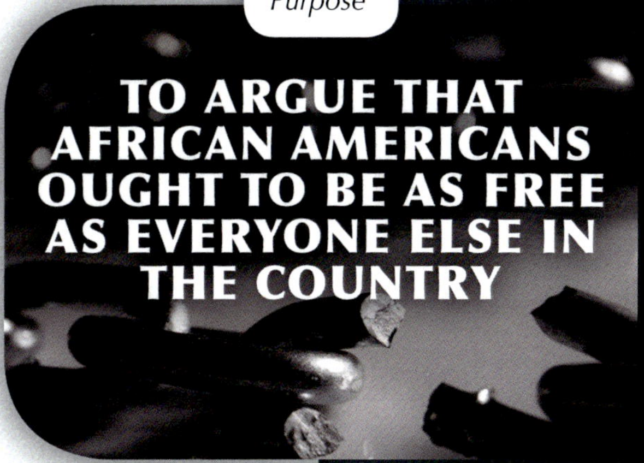

Place it was delivered

Maker's point of view

IN PRINT

A transcript is a printed version of a speech. In the 1800s, they were often written as the words were spoken or later from memory. Without audio or video recordings, transcripts may be the only form of a historical speech available to study. Douglass had copies of his speech ready for people to buy after the event. These transcripts showed what he intended to present. This means they can be trusted.

BEHIND THE WORDS

Transcripts of the speech list Frederick Douglass as the maker. In the speech itself, he said, "This, for the purpose of this celebration, is the 4th of July." This has caused confusion, because the speech was given on July 5. Printed copies confirm this date. The speech also referred to the setting as the Corinthian Hall. Douglass spoke about who was in the audience, too. He seemed to be familiar with many of them. He referred to someone as "Mr. President" but this was not the American president. Instead, this person would have been the leader of a group at the event.

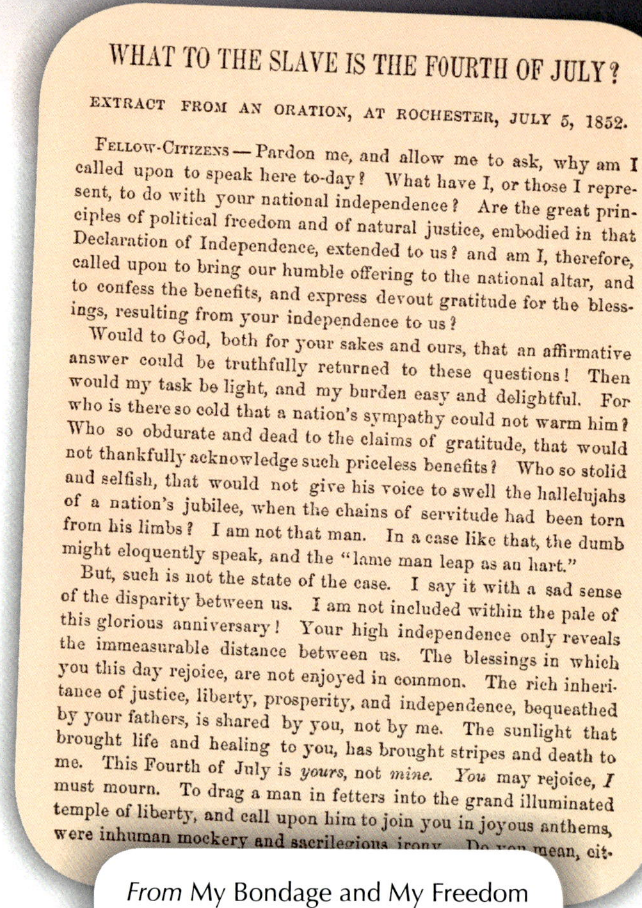

WHAT TO THE SLAVE IS THE FOURTH OF JULY?

EXTRACT FROM AN ORATION, AT ROCHESTER, JULY 5, 1852.

FELLOW-CITIZENS — Pardon me, and allow me to ask, why am I called upon to speak here to-day? What have I, or those I represent, to do with your national independence? Are the great principles of political freedom and of natural justice, embodied in that Declaration of Independence, extended to us? and am I, therefore, called upon to bring our humble offering to the national altar, and to confess the benefits, and express devout gratitude for the blessings, resulting from your independence to us?

Would to God, both for your sakes and ours, that an affirmative answer could be truthfully returned to these questions! Then would my task be light, and my burden easy and delightful. For who is there so cold that a nation's sympathy could not warm him? Who so obdurate and dead to the claims of gratitude, that would not thankfully acknowledge such priceless benefits? Who so stolid and selfish, that would not give his voice to swell the hallelujahs of a nation's jubilee, when the chains of servitude had been torn from his limbs? I am not that man. In a case like that, the dumb might eloquently speak, and the "lame man leap as an hart."

But, such is not the state of the case. I say it with a sad sense of the disparity between us. I am not included within the pale of this glorious anniversary! Your high independence only reveals the immeasurable distance between us. The blessings in which you this day rejoice, are not enjoyed in common. The rich inheritance of justice, liberty, prosperity, and independence, bequeathed by your fathers, is shared by you, not by me. The sunlight that brought life and healing to you, has brought stripes and death to me. This Fourth of July is *yours*, not *mine*. *You* may rejoice, *I* must mourn. To drag a man in fetters into the grand illuminated temple of liberty, and call upon him to join you in joyous anthems, were inhuman mockery and sacrilegious irony. Do you mean, cit-

From My Bondage and My Freedom *by Frederick Douglass*

Speaker: *Frederick Douglass*
Audience: *Abolitionists*
Date: *July 5, 1852*

> ***I will...dare to call in question and to denounce, with all the emphasis I can command, everything that serves to [enable] slavery—the great sin and shame of America!***
>
> ***I was born amid such sights and scenes. To me the American slave-trade is a terrible reality. When a child, my soul was often pierced with a sense of its horrors.***

Purpose of this speech

Douglass's personal experiences shaped his point of view

U.S. Library of Congress, Washington, D.C.

DATA CHECK

The basic details about a primary source may not be found in the source itself. For example, a speaker may not refer to the date or location. Libraries and other organizations gather information about the resources in their collections. It is entered into a catalog, or database. Reviewing this information can help confirm the facts.

The Frederick Douglass Papers at the Library of Congress is a collection of 7,400 papers, speeches, letters, and other material written by or about Frederick Douglass. Some of his early work was destroyed in a house fire in 1872.

TOOL FOR CHANGE

Like many speakers, Frederick Douglass pushed for change. He presented his side of an issue, which was usually ending slavery. His speeches were meant to sway an audience to think a certain way. His goal was to gain support. A few common features are found in most **persuasive** speeches like the one made by Douglass.

MAKING AN ARGUMENT

CLAIM

Speeches support their arguments with claims, which are statements or conclusions.

Schools should ban homework.

EVIDENCE

Evidence is data or facts that prove the claims are true.

Studies show no clear link between doing homework and getting higher marks.

WARRANT

Warrants connect claims and evidence to support a course of action.

To improve students' understanding of what they learn in school, we need to find better options than homework.

APPEAL

Appeals in speeches urge the audience to act.

Stop assigning homework today!

Use rhetorical language to strengthen the claims, evidence, and warrants in speeches.

INFLUENCING THE AUDIENCE

Rhetoric is used in speeches and many other texts. It is the art of **persuasion**. Like most speakers, Douglass used three main strategies in his speeches.

LOGOS

Logos relies on logic, or reason. In a speech, it may begin with a general idea that is supported by facts. Logos can also use facts as a starting point, then draw conclusions.

Students come from different backgrounds. They do not all have the same resources at home. Keeping schoolwork in the classroom means no one is at a disadvantage.

ETHOS

Ethos urges the audience to side with the speaker. It often depends on his or her good character. Showing respect, finding common ground, and sharing personal experiences are part of ethos.

As a teacher, I have found that giving homework does not raise grades. Therefore, I would like parents to consider whether it is worthwhile for their children.

PATHOS

Pathos plays on the audience's emotions to win them over.

Students today have more pressures on them than ever before. Their mental health would improve if they did not have to make time for homework every night.

WORDS THAT WORK

Douglass began studying rhetoric when he was a youth. One **biographer** called him "a genius with words." Rhetorical devices include:

- **Metaphors**, **similes**, and other figurative language
- Comparing two unalike things in an **analogy**
- Repeating key words and phrases
- Exaggerating in **hyperboles**
- Giving things human qualities through **personification**
- Making some facts sound less important than they really are

HEARD NOT READ

Speeches are meant to be delivered out loud. The experience is not the same when a speech is read silently. Language and voice are an important part of delivering a message to an audience. The way a speaker uses his or her voice can change how the listeners receive it.

DIGGING DEEPER

Do you think a speech could be persuasive without using rhetoric? Why or why not?

VOCAL POWER

Diction is the way someone pronounces and produces the sounds in words. Changing diction affects an audience even if the same words are spoken. It also includes the words a speaker or writer chooses to use. Emphasizing certain words helps stress a point. Cadence is the rising and falling rhythms of vocal tones. They can also help to alter a message.

VOICE CLUES

There are many photos of Douglass but no audio or video files of him giving speeches. Recording technologies, such as the phonograph, were not invented until later. However, secondary sources describe his speaking style. Douglass's voice was rich and deep. His tone was often fierce. He spoke with confidence. This came with a lot of practice. He worked on his skills while speaking at a church in New Bedford. He became an expert at keeping his audience's attention. The fact that this information is known today reveals his position of importance.

phonograph

Douglass studied persuasive speakers. He believed that speeches had more power than the written word. Here he is depicted giving his London Reception speech in England in 1846.

DIGGING DEEPER

Other than audio recordings, which other modern formats were not available in 1852? How could they make it easier to study a speech now?

CHAPTER 2

WORDS AND MEANING

Deconstructing a speech involves analyzing it in a detailed way. The first step is to review the whole source carefully. Look at both the information and how it is presented. Frederick Douglass used the parts of an argument and the rhetorical language described in the last chapter. They help him explain why enslaved people had no reason to celebrate on Independence Day.

ORGANIZING IDEAS

Speakers present their ideas in a variety of ways. Placing them in order is called sequencing. Frederick Douglass did this as he listed the events leading to the creation of the United States. He also used comparison and contrast in his argument. For example, Douglass compared the actions of the **founding fathers** in 1776 with the abolitionists of his day. Another use of this comparative style linked Britain's handling of **colonists** to how Americans treated enslaved people. Douglass also contrasted the character and motives of the country's first leaders to its current politicians. Douglass used the causal style in his speech, too. This describes causes and effects, such as why the colonies fought for freedom from British rule and the results.

PURPOSE

The purpose of a speech is the reason for making it. Douglass had an unusual goal with his Independence Day **address**. He urged the audience to see that there was no reason to celebrate the country's freedom until slavery was ended. Douglass likely upset some listeners when he declared, "There is not a nation on the earth guilty of practices, more shocking and bloody, than are the people of these United States..." He delivered a powerful argument that enslaved people must be freed.

DECONSTRUCT IT

To determine the purpose of a speech, listen to it or read it and ask:

- What is the speaker's main argument?
- Who is the speaker trying to appeal to?

Speaker: *Frederick Douglass*
Audience: *Abolitionists*
Date: *July 5, 1852*

"*What, to the American slave, is your* ***4th of July****? I answer: a day that reveals to him... the* ***gross injustice*** *and cruelty to which he is the constant victim...* ***your shouts of*** *liberty* ***and equality, hollow mockery****...*"

Refers to Independence Day celebrations

Obvious unfairness

These ideals are central to the Declaration of Independence; however, they did not apply to everyone

SPEAKER SPOTLIGHT

Frederick Douglass wrote for and created multiple newspapers. *The North Star* was the first one he published. Under its title on the front page was written: "RIGHT IS OF NO SEX—TRUTH IS OF NO COLOR—GOD IS THE FATHER OF US ALL, AND ALL WE ARE BRETHREN". This statement sums up the purpose of many of his speeches and written work. Getting equality for all people was his main goal. Douglass often appealed directly to religious groups. He believed they held enough power to sway the whole country.

THE NORTH STAR.

FREDERICK DOUGLASS, M. R. DELANY, Editors.

RIGHT IS OF NO SEX—TRUTH IS OF NO COLOR—GOD IS THE FATHER OF US ALL, AND ALL WE ARE BRETHREN.

WILLIAM C. NELL, Publisher. JOHN DICK, Printer.

VOL. I. NO. XI. ROCHESTER, N. Y., FRIDAY, MARCH 10, 1848. WHOLE NO.—XI.

Douglass became the editor of The North Star *newspaper in 1848.*

CLAIMS AND EVIDENCE

Frederick Douglass backed his argument with claims. He used evidence to support his conclusions. These statements and facts were influenced by the time period, setting, and audience. Most of the people at the event hosted by the Rochester Ladies' Anti-Slavery Society agreed with Douglass. However, the audience was mainly white American citizens. Their lives in 1852 were very different from those of enslaved people. He drew their attention to the inequality.

DECONSTRUCT IT

To find claims and evidence in a speech, ask:

- What conclusions are being made?
- Which facts or data support these statements?
- Does the speaker use voice, such as emphasis or pacing, to reinforce any text?

Speaker: *Frederick Douglass*
Audience: *Abolitionists*
Date: *July 5, 1852*

> ***There are seventy-two crimes in the State of Virginia, which, if committed by a black man…subject him to the punishment of death…What is this but the acknowledgment that the slave is a moral, intellectual, and responsible being?***

The speech included facts such as numbers, dates, and places that could be confirmed

Douglass's claims led the audience to conclude that his argument simply made sense

DIGGING DEEPER

When there are no recordings of a speech, it is difficult to know how a speaker used diction or tone. In what ways could Douglass have used his voice to sway the audience?

WARRANTS AND APPEALS

Appeals in speeches ask the audience to take action or change the way they think. Frederick Douglass urged them to view enslaved people as humans like all others who had the right to the freedoms being celebrated on the Fourth of July. This knowledge would help end slavery. Douglass linked claims and evidence in warrants to support this appeal. Warrants are statements that support a course of action.

DECONSTRUCT IT

Find warrants and appeals in a speech by asking:

- Is the speaker urging the audience to act or think a certain way?
- How are claims and evidence being connected to convince them?

Speaker: *Frederick Douglass*
Audience: *Abolitionists*
Date: *July 5, 1852*

"***With brave men there is always a remedy for oppression…It was a startling idea…*** *some were, of course, shocked and alarmed by it. Such people lived then, had lived before, and will, probably, ever have a place on this planet…* ***They hate all changes, but silver, gold and copper change***!"

Calls the audience to be part of the solution

Breaking free from Britain

Cleverly suggests that greed is the real reason why slavery existed

BEHIND THE WORDS

Douglass urged the audience to compare themselves to those who started the **American Revolution**. Colonists in the 1760s did not know whether their fight against Britain would succeed. They had to be brave and take risks for a better future. People listening to Douglass had their own choice to make. They could be bold and act or be like those who would have stayed under British rule. This was very effective since the speech was given right after Independence Day.

Americans won their freedom from British rule at the end of the American Revolutionary War in 1783.

Frederick Douglass was a compelling speaker and his ideas angered supporters of slavery who wanted to protect their advantages and keep people in chains. The 1860 abolitionist meeting in Boston where he gave a speech was shut down when anti-abolitionists disrupted it and called the police.

SPEAKER SPOTLIGHT

Frederick Douglass delivered a speech to another group of abolitionists on December 3, 1860. They were gathered at the Tremont Temple in Boston to discuss the best way to end slavery. Douglass urged them to rise up against slave owners. He reviewed some of the arguments that others had made in the past. He noted that horrifying images, such as "men tied to the stake and deliberately burned, the blood gushing from their nose and eyes, asking rather to be shot than to be murdered by such slow torture" had not been enough to move Americans. He described them as "indifferent to these cries for deliverance," or freedom. Douglass argued that slave owners were becoming harder to sway despite the overwhelming facts. He urged the audience "not only to appeal to the moral sense of these slaveholders; we have need, and a right, to appeal to their fears."

ARTFUL RHETORIC

At the beginning of Frederick Douglass's speech, he noted that he was a long way from his start in life as an enslaved person. He said, "With little experience and with less learning, I have been able to throw my thoughts hastily and imperfectly together." This was an understatement of his skills. Douglass studied rhetoric and was known for being an accomplished speaker. His speech used a variety of devices, such as analogies. In one, he compared the United States to a young child whose destiny is not yet set. Douglass also used repetition to great effect. The word "chains" appears throughout his speech. It highlights the lack of freedom that enslaved people faced. Douglass's speech also showed that he was familiar with literature as well as history. He quoted *Julius Caesar*, a play by William Shakespeare. His mastery of language and persuasion is seen throughout "What to the Slave Is the Fourth of July?"

Frederick Douglass admired Harriet Tubman. She was an abolitionist and a Union army spy.

Harriet Tubman (far left) escaped slavery in 1849, when she was 27 years old. She then led hundreds of enslaved people, including her parents and several siblings, out of bondage via the Underground Railroad. Although she never learned to read or write, she knew the power of words and stories. She collaborated with authors who wrote about her, using the money earned from her life stories to rescue and support others.

DECONSTRUCT IT

To identify the rhetorical language in a speech, ask:

- How is the speaker using logic and reason to persuade the audience?
- Does the speaker's character help support the central argument?
- How is the audience being swayed by emotion?

Speaker: *Frederick Douglass*
Audience: *Abolitionists*
Date: *July 5, 1852*

Douglass used ethos and built trust when he showed respect for the founding fathers of the United States

> “***The signers of the Declaration of Independence were brave men…*** *patriots* ***and heroes, and for the good they did, and the principles they contended for, I will unite with you to honor their memory.***”

Key Founding Fathers

John Adams

Benjamin Franklin

Alexander Hamilton

John Jay

Thomas Jefferson

James Madison

George Washington

*Is it not astonishing that, while we are **ploughing, planting and reaping, using all kinds of mechanical tools, erecting houses, constructing bridges, building ships**...**acting as clerks, merchants and secretaries, having among us lawyers, doctors, ministers, poets, authors, editors, orators and teachers**...**thinking, planning, living in families as husbands, wives and children**...we are called upon to prove that we are men!*

*...am I to argue that it is wrong to make men brutes...**to work them without wages...to beat them with sticks...to hunt them with dogs, to sell them at auction**...**to knock out their teeth, to burn their flesh, to starve them into obedience**...?*

In this example of logos, a long list of facts clearly supports Douglass's conclusion that enslaved people are humans

Douglass's examples sparked pathos and played on his audience's emotions

Speaker: *Frederick Douglass*
Audience: *Abolitionists*
Date: *July 5, 1852*

African American men fought in the Civil War. African Americans, both free and enslaved, fought in the War of Independence as well.

SPEAKER SPOTLIGHT

Frederick Douglass gave another important speech on July 6, 1863. This was during the American Civil War. The **Union army** had won the Battle of Gettysburg just three days earlier. There were over 5,000 people in the audience at the National Hall in Philadelphia. Douglass focused on the African American men in the crowd. His purpose was to convince them to fight the **Confederates**. He posed the question about the two sides: "...which is for us, and which against us"? Douglass used logos to reason that this was the only opportunity to seize their rights. By sharing common ground with them he employed ethos. Through pathos, Douglass fired them up to go to war. He claimed that the soldiers from the South were fighting for "the horrid privilege...of trafficking in slaves and the souls of men; for the ghastly privilege of... selling innocent children." Arguments such as this one encouraged 180,000 African American men to serve as soldiers in the Civil War.

DIGGING DEEPER

How do you think we should react to terms in historical speeches that are now considered offensive?

ANALYZING PERSPECTIVES

Frederick Douglass often spoke about ending slavery in the United States. He was passionate about it because of his personal experiences. His speeches showed his perspective, or point of view. They also revealed what American society in the 1800s thought about the issue. Douglass wrote his own speeches. Sometimes, a writer creates a speech on behalf of the person who delivers it. The writer aims to present the speaker's perspective.

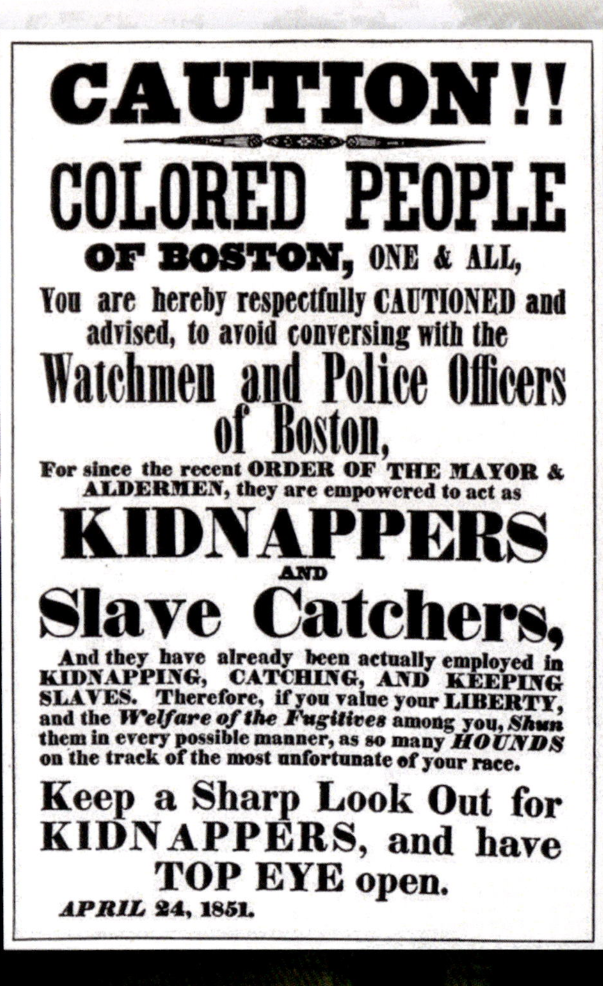

CAUTION!!

COLORED PEOPLE

OF BOSTON, ONE & ALL,

You are hereby respectfully CAUTIONED and advised, to avoid conversing with the

Watchmen and Police Officers of Boston,

For since the recent ORDER OF THE MAYOR & ALDERMEN, they are empowered to act as

KIDNAPPERS

AND

Slave Catchers,

And they have already been actually employed in KIDNAPPING, CATCHING, AND KEEPING SLAVES. Therefore, if you value your LIBERTY, and the *Welfare of the Fugitives* among you, *Shun* them in every possible manner, as so many *HOUNDS* on the track of the most unfortunate of your race.

Keep a Sharp Look Out for KIDNAPPERS, and have TOP EYE open.

APRIL 24, 1851.

The Fugitive Slave Act meant fugitives, or escapees, from slavery could be captured in any state.

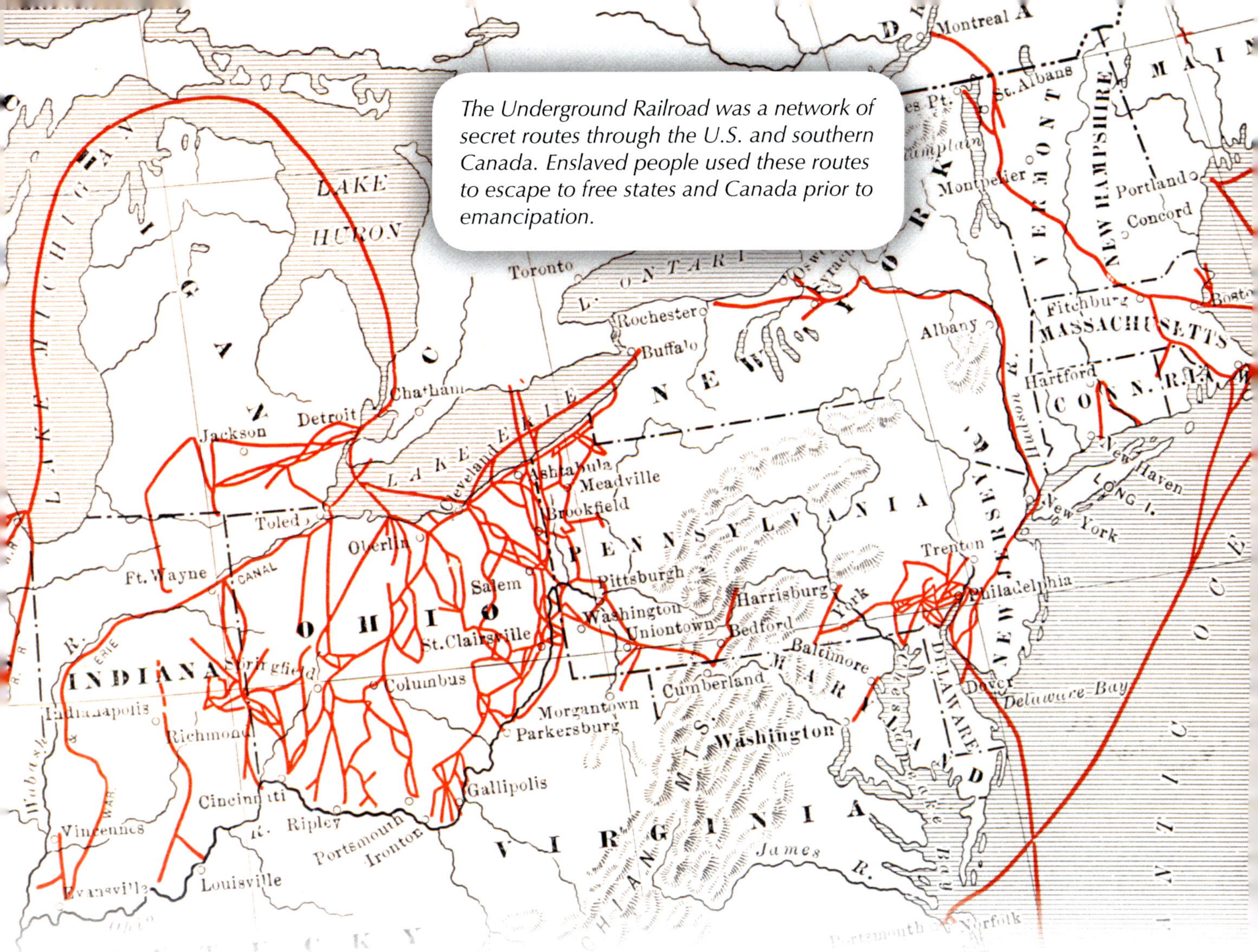

The Underground Railroad was a network of secret routes through the U.S. and southern Canada. Enslaved people used these routes to escape to free states and Canada prior to emancipation.

A DIVIDED COUNTRY

The time in history when a speech is made also affects its point of view. The maker and the audience are influenced by their era. In 1852, the United States was less than 100 years old. Civil war was looming. Differing views on slavery threatened to tear apart the country. The United States Congress had recently passed the *Fugitive Slave Act*. Douglass described it in his speech. He said, "the power to hold, hunt, and sell men, women, and children as slaves…is now an institution of the whole United States… The Fugitive Slave Law makes mercy to them a crime…" Having escaped from slavery, Douglass knew the fear of being captured.

FLIGHT TO FREEDOM

Thousands of enslaved people were fleeing the southern states at that time. Frederick and Anna Douglass were part of the Underground Railroad. This was a secret network of routes and homes that led to freedom in the north. Abolitionists and others used them to help people escape from slavery. The Douglass family may have assisted up to 400 fugitives from slavery. Hearing their stories encouraged Frederick to continue the fight. He also knew that even free Black people faced constant racism and threats to their lives. They would not be citizens with rights for another 14 years.

REVEALING LANGUAGE

The words speechmakers use can highlight their perspective. Frederick Douglass called the audience "fellow citizens" twice in his speech. As an a Black man, Douglass could not be a citizen of the United States—it was not yet a birthright. This was no mistake on his part. He drew attention to it on purpose. Douglass stirred up people's emotions with his loaded words. He also swayed them with **nuanced** language. For example, he emphasized the divide between himself and many in the audience when he spoke about Independence Day as "yours" instead of "ours."

DECONSTRUCT IT

To examine a speaker's perspective, ask:

- How does the language used show the speaker's feelings?
- How could the speaker's point of view be summed up in one sentence?

Speaker: *Frederick Douglass*
Audience: *Abolitionists*
Date: *July 5, 1852*

"*I shall see, **this day**...from the slave's point of view...**I do not hesitate to declare, with all my soul, that the character and conduct of this nation never looked blacker to me than on this 4th of July**!*"

Independence Day

Douglass made his perspective clear. He also called the actions of the United States "hideous and revolting."

Artist John Lewis Krimmel's painting Independence Day Celebration in Centre Square, Philadelphia, *from 1819. Krimmel was a German American immigrant who enjoyed all the freedoms enslaved people could not.*

A SINGLE VIEW

Speeches and other primary sources often present only one point of view. Frederick Douglass knew that at least some of the audience would not side with him. His perspective on Independence Day was shocking. Even abolitionists disagreed on various points. Others in the crowd probably disagreed with his rhetoric. In fact, he noted, "I fancy I hear some one of my audience say...Would you argue more, and denounce less, would you persuade more, and rebuke less, your cause would be much more likely to succeed." Focusing on only one perspective limits what can be learned about an issue. Speakers may leave out facts that work against his or her argument, for example.

DECONSTRUCT IT

To find the limitations of a speech, ask:

- How does the maker's perspective shape this primary source?
- Are any important facts being left out?
- Based on evidence from other sources, are there any points that should be explored further?
- How are edits important?

BEHIND THE WORDS

Frederick Douglass was very familiar with the arguments for and against slavery. He knew how people who were pro-slavery would counter his claims. Douglass used this to his advantage in his speech. He referred to so-called "evidence" and then explained the facts as he saw them. For example, many slave owners argued that Black people were not fully human. Douglass refuted this ridiculous idea. Some of the best evidence was his own life and his powerful speech.

Speaker: *Frederick Douglass*
Audience: *Abolitionists*
Date: *July 5, 1852*

"*Must I undertake to prove that the slave is a man?...It is admitted in the fact that* ***Southern statute books are covered with enactments forbidding, under severe fines and penalties, the teaching of the slave to read or to write.*** *When you can point to any such laws,* ***in reference to the beasts of the field****, then I may...argue the manhood of the slave.*"

Described state government orders making it against the law to educate enslaved people

If the South really thought enslaved people were animals, Douglass questioned why these laws did not also apply to animals

SPEAKER SPOTLIGHT

In 1857, Dred Scott went to court in the hope of freeing himself and his family from slavery. The U.S. Supreme Court ruled against him. Frederick Douglass spoke to the American Anti-Slavery Society about it in New York on May 14 that year. He argued that there was more than one way to view the court's decision. Instead of losing faith in the cause, Douglass urged, "In one point of view, we, the abolitionists and colored people, should meet this decision, unlooked for and monstrous as it appears, in a cheerful spirit. This very attempt to blot out forever the hopes of an enslaved people may be one necessary link in the chain of events...to the downfall and complete overthrow of the whole slave system." He saw the denial of Scott's freedom as a step forward in ending slavery.

In 1857, the U.S. Supreme Court ruled that Dred Scott was not a citizen with rights.

OTHER PERSPECTIVES

Every person has a point of view. Secondary sources reveal many perspectives and **biases**. This means the same speech could be deconstructed in multiple ways. Studying a variety of sources leads to a greater understanding of an issue. These materials could be from the same time period. They could also look at a speech from a modern perspective.

DIGGING DEEPER

How do people's different backgrounds influence their perspectives?

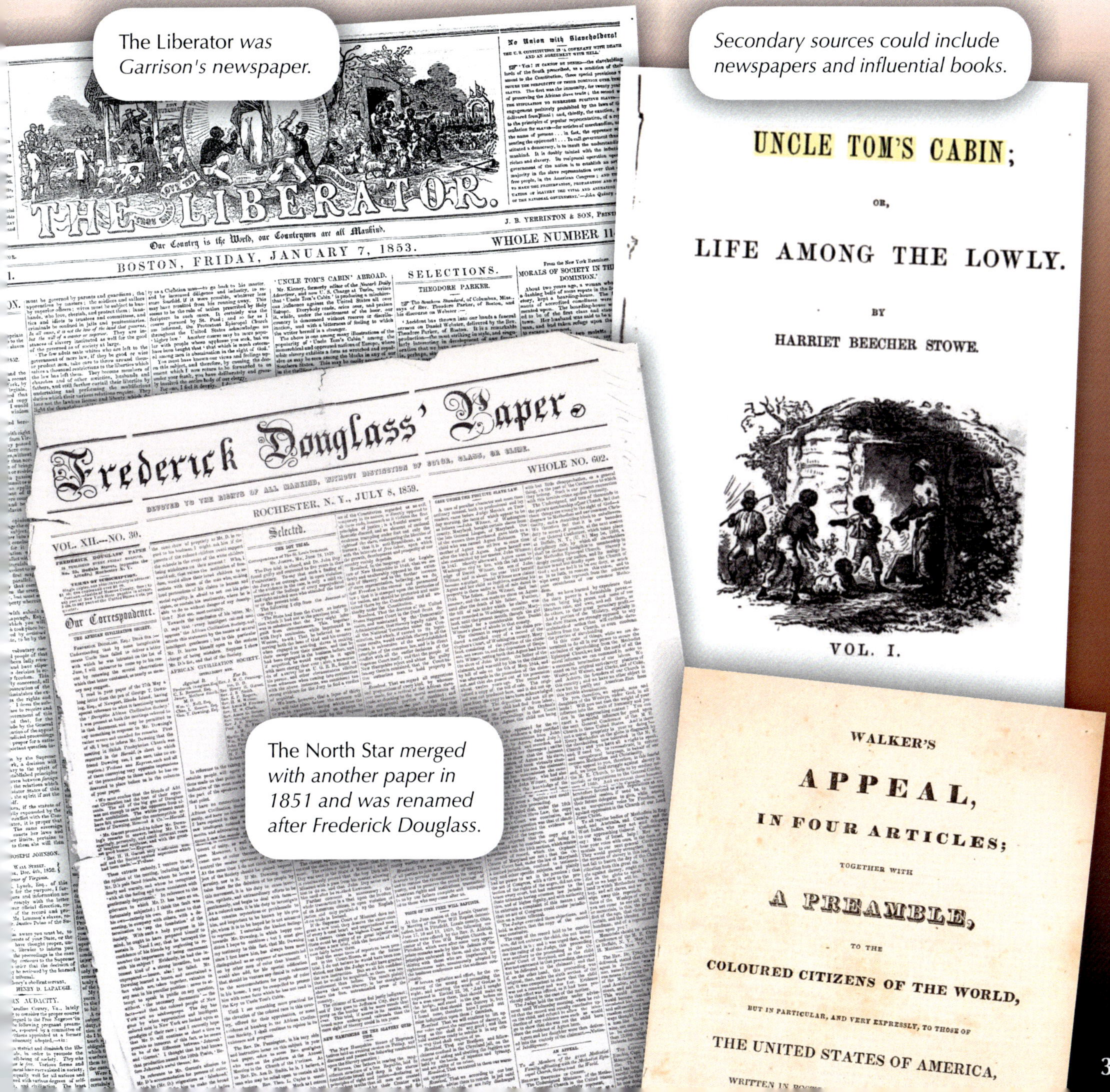

THE LIBERATOR.

Our Country is the World, our Countrymen are all Mankind.

BOSTON, FRIDAY, JANUARY 7, 1853.

WHOLE NUMBER 11

No Union with Slaveholders!

Frederick Douglass' Paper.

DEVOTED TO THE RIGHTS OF ALL MANKIND, WITHOUT DISTINCTION OF COLOR, CLASS, OR CLIME.

ROCHESTER, N.Y., JULY 8, 1859.

VOL. XII.—NO. 30.

WHOLE NO. 602.

UNCLE TOM'S CABIN;

OR,

LIFE AMONG THE LOWLY.

BY

HARRIET BEECHER STOWE.

VOL. I.

WALKER'S

APPEAL,

IN FOUR ARTICLES;

TOGETHER WITH

A PREAMBLE,

TO THE

COLOURED CITIZENS OF THE WORLD,

BUT IN PARTICULAR, AND VERY EXPRESSLY, TO THOSE OF

THE UNITED STATES OF AMERICA,

The Liberator was Garrison's newspaper.

Secondary sources could include newspapers and influential books.

The North Star merged with another paper in 1851 and was renamed after Frederick Douglass.

THE "MUDSILL THEORY"

Many Americans did not share Frederick Douglass's point of view. This included powerful politicians, such as James Henry Hammond. He delivered a speech to the United States Senate on March 4, 1858. Leaders from across the country were in the audience at the U.S. Capitol in Washington, D.C. Hammond believed that upper **classes** needed people below them. This lower level was like the mudsill, or base, that supported a building. He claimed that in northern states, white people were forced to take on roles that were suited to enslaved people. He argued that it was better to have "happy" enslaved people from an "inferior" race. His perspective that enslaved people were lesser beings was in stark contrast with Frederick Douglass's speech.

James Henry Hammond was the Governor of South Carolina and later a U.S. Senator.

Speaker: *Henry Hammond*
Audience: *Leaders from across the U.S.A.*
Date: *March 4, 1858*

> *In all social systems* ***there must be a class to do the menial duties, to perform the drudgery of life****...Such a class you must have, or you would not have that* ***other class which leads progress,*** *civilization,* ***and refinement****... Fortunately for the South,* ***she found a race adapted to that purpose****...*

This is still seen today as certain groups are more likely to work hard at low-skilled jobs

Hammond clearly viewed his own class and race as superior and worthy to lead

The slave trade kidnapped about half a million Africans and shipped them to America. Hammond rationalized that Africans were more suited to slavery because this belief suited his aims.

Douglass might agree with Hammond that the labors of enslaved people laid the foundation of the U.S.

READ IT

The full text of Hammond's speech is available at **www.pbs.org/wgbh/aia/part4/4h3439t.html**

A WOMAN OF ACTION

Like Frederick Douglass, Mary Ann Shadd Cary published a newspaper. She also agreed with his views on abolition. However, the two had different ideas about how to end slavery. Cary once told Douglass, "We should do more and talk less." When the *Fugitive Slave Act* was passed, she and her family moved to North Buxton in what is now Ontario, Canada. Slavery was abolished there in 1834. While there, Cary worked toward **integration** in schools. She believed that the races should be educated together. Cary also helped with the Underground Railroad. She encouraged African Americans to settle in Canada.

Mary Ann Shadd Cary was also a teacher and a lawyer.

Provincial Freeman.

DEVOTED TO ANTI-SLAVERY, TEMPERANCE, AND GENERAL LITERATURE.

"Self-Reliance is the True Road to Independence."

SAMUEL R. WARD, Editor. ALEX. M'ARTHUR, Cor. Editor.

TORONTO, CANADA WEST, SATURDAY, SEPTEMBER 9, 1854.

VOL. I.—NO. 25.

PROSPECTUS OF THE PROVINCIAL FREEMAN,

Poetry.

The Birth of Christ.

Miscellaneous.

Interesting Discoveries in Naples.

JOB PRINTING!

Business Directory.

CHARLES MARCH

A. B. JONES,

D. FARRAR, & CO.,

Literature.

Borneo.

THE CHINESE SCHOOL.

Hindoo Belief.

THE PRESS.

Shadd Cary founded The Provincial Freeman *in 1853 and became the first Black woman editor and publisher in North America. She was critical of abolitionists who did not fight for full equality.*

A DIFFERENT FIGHT

Mary Ann Shadd Cary faced a huge problem because of the era in which she lived. Some people thought slavery should be ended—but did not believe in equal rights for women. In October 1855, the Colored National Convention was held in Philadelphia. Most of the group assembled at the Franklin Hall were free African American men. The official notes reveal that there was "a spirited discussion" about allowing Miss Mary A. Shadd to speak about the opportunities to be had in Canada. The vote was "Yeas, 38—Nays, 23." Mr. F. Douglass was listed as supporting her. She became the first woman ever to speak at the convention. As a sign of those times, no one bothered to write a transcript of what she actually said. However, Douglass's newspaper reported about it soon after.

African Americans met at conventions around the country. They discussed abolition, their rights, and the future.

"*[Mary Ann Shadd Cary]* **at first had ten minutes granted...ten more were granted**...**so interested was the House**, *that it granted additional time to her to finish...the House was crowded and breathless in its attention to her* **masterly exposition of our present condition**..."

Source: *Frederick Douglass's Paper*
Audience: *Readers across the U.S.*
Date: *October 26, 1855*

Given that many men voted against her speaking, it was worth noting that she was given more than double her allotted time

Referred to the convention attendees

She skillfully described the issues facing African Americans

DIGGING DEEPER

Do you think everyone is treated equally in today's society? Why or why not?

INFLUENCES THEN AND NOW

The audience was receptive to "What to the Slave Is the Fourth of July?" Frederick Douglass printed transcripts of the speech text in advance. He sold 700 copies at the Corinthian Hall that day. His newspaper also printed his speech, which helped it reach a much wider audience. Douglass continued to tour the country and argue against slavery. He became America's leading abolitionist and his words helped sway people into taking action.

LATER LIFE

In 1859, Frederick Douglass was connected with a plot to start a slave **rebellion**. He escaped to Canada to avoid being caught. From there, he traveled to England. Douglass continued speaking out against slavery wherever he went. He was back in the United States during the Civil War in the early 1860s. Douglass celebrated the end of slavery with the 13th Amendment in 1865. During his lifetime, he also saw African Americans get the right to citizenship and voting rights with the 14th and 15th Amendments. In 1872, Douglass moved to Washington, D.C. He held many political posts. It was unusual for an African American to hold this kind of power in that era. Douglass used his authority to keep fighting for equality for all.

Douglass's home at Cedar Hill, Washington D.C., became a National Historic Site. It hosts an annual speech contest for students.

Frederick Douglass with his second wife, Helen (seated), and her sister Eva Pitts.

FINAL YEARS

Anna Douglass died in 1882. A couple of years later, Frederick married Helen Pitts. She was a younger, white woman. Their relationship was very controversial at the time. Douglass kept working until his death by a heart attack on February 20, 1895. The 77-year-old went to a National Council of Women meeting that day and had planned to speak at a church later on. He never gave up on fighting for the causes he believed in.

DIGGING DEEPER

Most modern versions of Douglass's speech are shortened. What are the potential problems with cutting out some of his words?

THEN AND NOW

In his Independence Day speech, Frederick Douglass noted, "Were the nation older, the patriot's heart might be sadder..." The United States was still young and finding its way. He had hope for its future. The country is 167 years older now. African Americans have won full freedom and rights. However, racism and the **legacy** of slavery have yet to be defeated. In 1852, Douglass exposed the bias of his fellow Americans. He called them "remarkably familiar with all facts which make in their own favor. This is [prized] by some as a national trait—perhaps a national weakness." The question is whether these values have changed. Douglass knew the danger of celebrating the good without facing the bad.

MODERN PERSPECTIVES

Frederick Douglass's speech continues to make an impact. On Independence Day in 2019, football player Colin Kaepernick used an excerpt of "What to the Slave Is the Fourth of July?" in a video appeal. He had been trying to convince Nike not to release a special shoe. The shoe's design had Betsy Ross's American flag on it. This version of the flag was created during the era of slavery, and some racist groups have more recently adopted it as a symbol. In a Twitter tweet, Kaepernick paired Douglass's rhetoric with modern technology. The video showed disturbing images and video clips depicting real life incidents of racist violence. These were shown as famous African American actor James Earl Jones read parts of the speech. They highlighted historical and ongoing contemporary violence against Black Americans. Kaepernick's Twitter post got over four million views. Not everyone shared Kaepernick's perspective, though. Texas Senator Ted Cruz responded on Twitter. He claimed the speech was being used to argue something that Douglass did not intend. This sparked social media debate. In the end, Kaepernick persuaded Nike to pull the shoe.

This early American flag has been used by racist groups because of its connection to a time when slavery was legal.

Some people questioned whether Ted Cruz, a white man, should speak on behalf of Frederick Douglass.

Colin Kaepernick is known for refusing to stand during the national anthem. It is his protest against racial inequality in America.

DIGGING DEEPER

Do you think an argument made in a video produced for social media could be as convincing as one delivered in person? Why or why not?

"THE CASE FOR REPARATIONS"

One of the issues that the Kaepernick-Cruz debate brought up is that Americans still view slavery very differently. Some think of it as over and done with. Others believe that it continues to be "the great sin and shame of America" as Frederick Douglass called it. In June 2014, author and journalist Ta-Nehisi Coates wrote "The Case for Reparations" for *Atlantic* magazine. The article described the ripple effects of slavery that are still felt today. Its purpose was to argue in favor of **reparations** being made to the descendants of enslaved Africans. This would be a step toward correcting some of the wrongs of the past. Coates sparked new interest in whether reparations could pay for what he called the country's "moral debts." On June 19, 2019, he addressed a U.S. Congress committee about it.

Ta-Nehisi Coates joined others in arguing for reparations before a Congress committee.

Enslavement reigned for 250 years on these shores. When it ended, this country could have extended its ***hallowed principles—life, liberty, and the pursuit of happiness****—to all, regardless of color.* ***But America had other principles in mind****. And so for a century after the Civil War, black people were subjected to a* ***relentless campaign of terror****…* ***this body has a chance to…reject fair-weather patriotism, to say that this nation is both its credits and debits…***

Speaker: *Ta-Nehisi Coates*
Audience: *U.S. Congress committee*
Date: *June 19, 2019*

Referred to the Declaration of Independence

Questioned the country's values

African Americans faced racism and abuses of their rights in every aspect of life

Appealed to Congress to own up to the good and the bad parts of American history and take action to make amends

WATCH IT

See Ta-Nehisi Coates address Congress: **www.youtube.com/watch?v=kcCnQ3iRkys**

LASTING LEGACY

The question of whether equality has really been achieved remains. That is why Frederick Douglass's speech is still relevant today. Groups around the United States read it around July 4 each year. It is a reminder of the contrast between everyday life for many Americans and the ideals for which the United States stands.

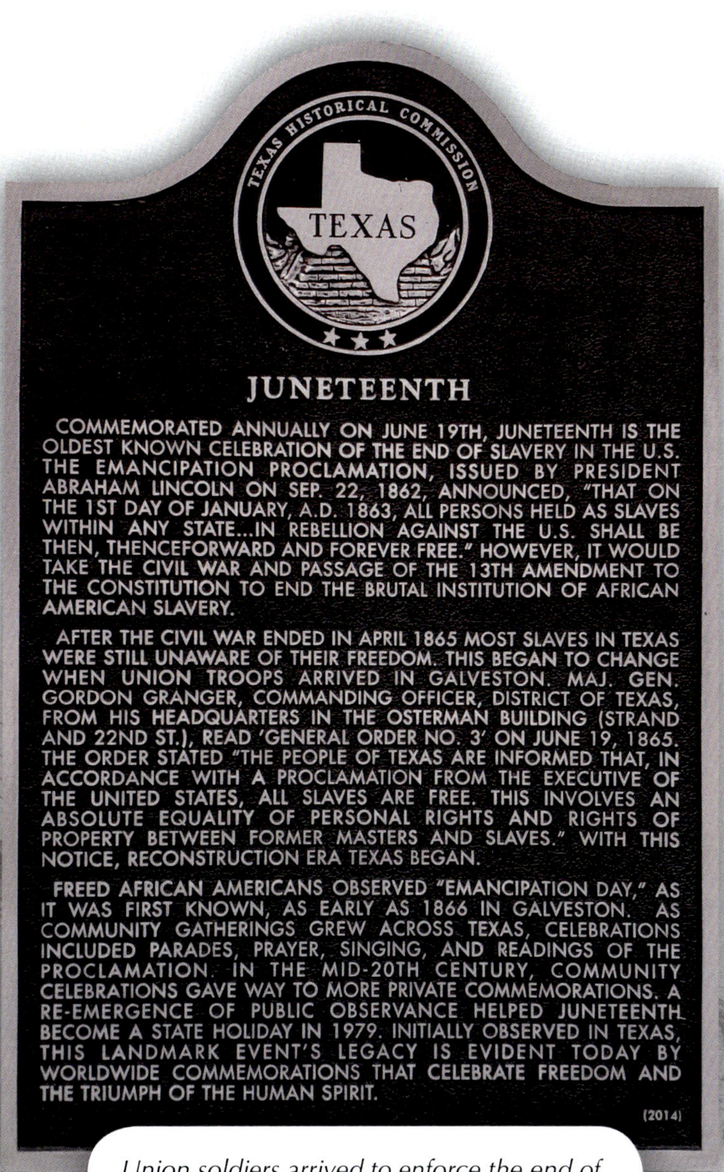

Union soldiers arrived to enforce the end of slavery in Texas on June 19, 1865. The date is now a state holiday called Juneteenth.

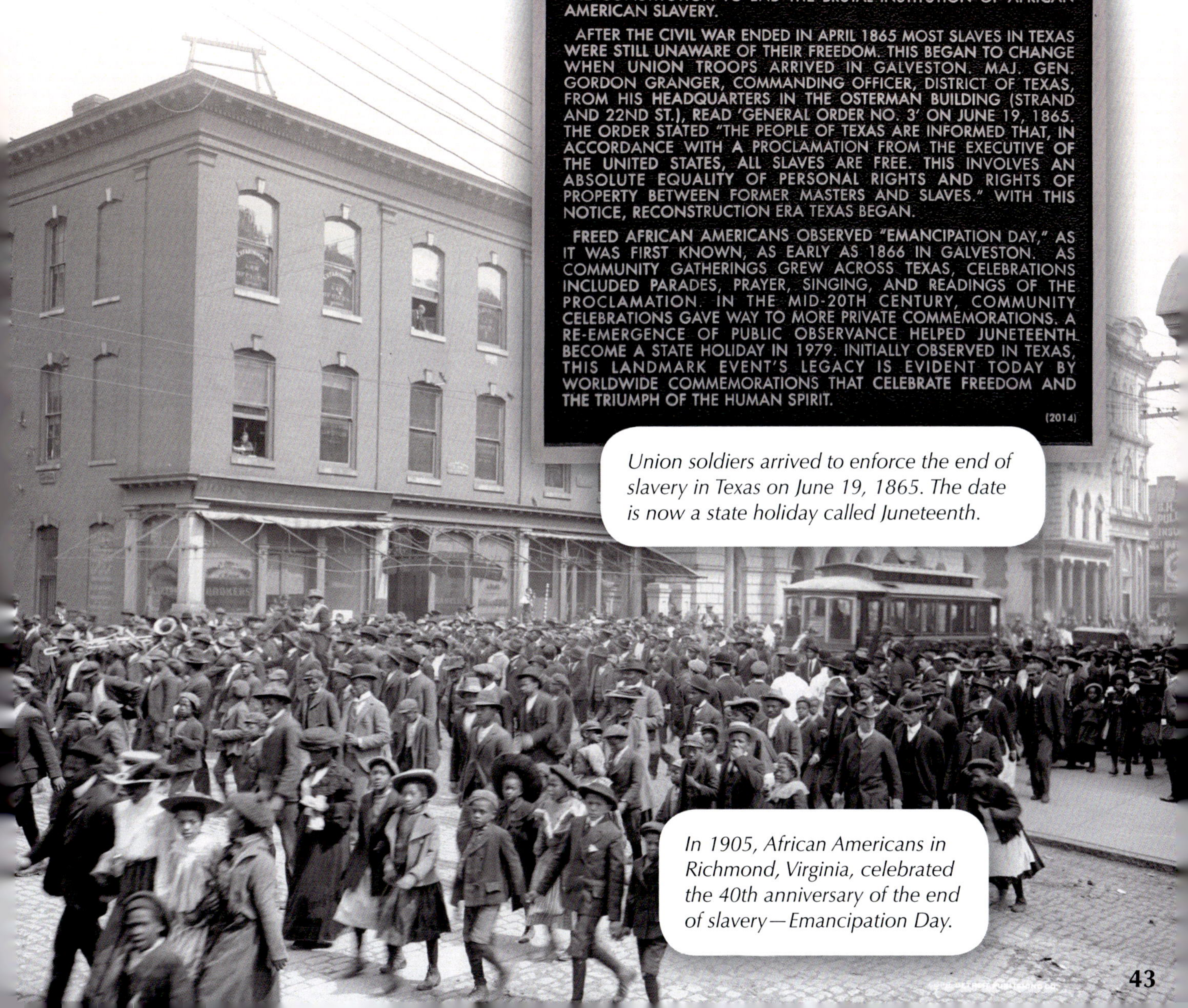

In 1905, African Americans in Richmond, Virginia, celebrated the 40th anniversary of the end of slavery—Emancipation Day.

BIBLIOGRAPHY

INTRODUCTION

Davidson, James West. "The Best Fourth of July Speech in American History." *Slate*, July 2, 2015. https://bit.ly/3eGQ8GP

Douglass, Frederick. *The Life and Times of Frederick Douglass*. Hartford: Park Publishing, 1881.

Douglass, Frederick. *Narrative of the Life of Frederick Douglass, an American Slave*. London: H.G. Collins, 1851.

Foner, Philip, and Yuval Taylor, eds. *Frederick Douglass: Selected Speeches and Writings*. Chicago: Chicago Review Press, 2000.

"Frederick Douglass." Library of Congress. www.loc.gov/item/today-in-history/september-03

"Frederick Douglass." National Park Service. https://bit.ly/2KoxhCI

"Frederick Douglass and the Columbian Orator." The Buckley School. https://bit.ly/3bttOyq

Gatewood, Willard B. "An 'African Prince, Majestic in His Wrath': William S. McFeely's Biography of Frederick Douglass." *The Florida Historical Quarterly*, October 1991. https://bit.ly/3alQ6ks

Powell, Jim. "Frederick Douglass: Heroic Orator for Liberty." Foundation for Economic Education. https://bit.ly/3eF8BUp

"Slavery." Frederick Douglass Family Initiatives. www.fdfi.org/slavery.html

Staples, Brent. "Frederick Douglass in Full." *The New York Times*, November 5, 2018. nyti.ms/33oYCvq

Sterngass, Jon. *Frederick Douglass*. New York: Infobase Publishing, 2014.

Strauss, Valerie. "Why an 1852 speech by Frederick Douglass should be taught to students today." *The Washington Post*, July 4, 2019. wapo.st/2OJ0H02

Zirin, Dave. "'What to the Slave Is the Fourth of July?' by Frederick Douglass."

The Nation, July 4, 2012. www.thenation.com/article/what-slave-fourth-july-frederick-douglass

CHAPTER 1

Banks, Adelle M. "5 religious facts you might not know about Frederick Douglass." *The Washington Post*, June 19, 2013. wapo.st/2OTkda8

Beeson, Jennifer. "Who's the most photographed American man of the 19th Century? HINT: It's not Lincoln…" *The Washington Post*, March 15, 2016. wapo.st/2QXzNo2

"Development." Douglass: The Musical. www.douglassthemusical.com/development

Fahnestock, Jeanne. Rhetorical Style: *The Uses of Language in Persuasion*. New York: Oxford University Press, 2011.

"*Frederick Douglass: Prophet of Freedom* recasts the life of one of our major literary figures." Library of America. https://bit.ly/2RTDj28

"Picture This: Frederick Douglass Was The Most Photographed Man Of His Time." National Public Radio. n.pr/2OO3qFA

"Primary Sources." University of California Irvine Libraries. https://bit.ly/2KmsrFV

"Primary Sources: What Are They?" Teaching History. https://bit.ly/34RHIYI

"Primary vs. Secondary Sources." BMCC Library. lib1.bmcc.cuny.edu/help/sources

"Using Primary Sources." United States Library of Congress. https://bit.ly/2wZAi9u

Weida, Stacy, and Karl Stolley. "Using Rhetorical Strategies for Persuasion."

Purdue Online Writing Lab. https://bit.ly/2RWntUw

Wexler, Natalie. "Why Homework Doesn't Seem To Boost Learning—And How It Could." Forbes, January 3, 2019. https://bit.ly/3eCa6m9

CHAPTER 2

"Address at a Meeting for the Promotion of Colored Enlistments, Philadelphia." Library of Congress. www.loc.gov/item/mfd.22007

"Black Civil War Soldiers." History, A&E Television. https://bit.ly/2RWKalm

Douglass, Frederick. *Frederick Douglass on Slavery and the Civil War: Selections from His Writings*. Mineola: Dover Publications, 2003.

"Speech: 'Friends, Romans, countrymen, lend me your ears'." Poetry Foundation. https://bit.ly/3eE6T5v

"Speech on John Brown, delivered in Tremont Temple, Boston, December 3, 1860, by Frederick Douglass." Historical Society of Pennsylvania. https://bit.ly/34UyJ9t

"Students in Arms: The Institute for Colored Youth and the Civil War." Falvey Memorial Library, Villanova University. https://bit.ly/2VGHJL2

CHAPTER 3

Bizzell, Patricia. "The 4th of July and the 22nd of December: The Function of Cultural Archives in Persuasion, as Shown by Frederick Douglass and William Apess." *College Composition and Communication*. https://bit.ly/3buEihk

Douglass, Frederick. "The Dred Scott Decision." University of Rochester Frederick Douglass Project. https://rbscp.lib.rochester.edu/4399

Douglass, Frederick. "Country, Conscience, and the Anti-Slavery Cause." *New York Daily Tribune*, May 13, 1847. https://bit.ly/34RgvW6

Gates Jr., Henry Louis, and John Stauffer. "Five myths about Frederick Douglass." *The Washington Post*, February 10, 2017. https://wapo.st/2DEcmrY

Hammond, James Henry. "The Mudsill Theory." Africans in America. https://to.pbs.org/2KmMUKT

Logan, Shirley Wilson. *We Are Coming: The Persuasive Discourse of Nineteenth-Century Black Women*. Carbondale: Southern Illinois University Press, 1999.

"Mary Ann Shadd." The Canadian Encyclopedia. https://bit.ly/3eBwaxv

Tucker, Neely. "Mary Ann Shadd Cary: Trailblazer for Feminism, Freedom." Library of Congress. https://bit.ly/3cy4Myv

"Underground Railroad." History. https://bit.ly/2KpgLlL

CHAPTER 4

Coates, Ta-Nehisi. "The Case for Reparations." *The Atlantic*, June 2014. https://bit.ly/34SlDJG

"Frederick Douglass Timeline." Library of Congress. https://bit.ly/2VGGn2U

Giammona, Craig, Eben Novy-Williams, and Rob Golum. "Nike defends recall of Betsy Ross flag shoe that reopened culture-war rift." *Los Angeles Times*, July 2, 2019. www.lat.ms/2RFdXFY

Harvey, H. Michael. "Ted Cruz Stop Whitesplaining Frederick Douglass to Colin Kaepernick." Medium, July 6, 2019. https://bit.ly/2VS5lN0

Kaepernick, Colin (@Kaepernick7). "What have I, or those I represent, to do with your national independence?" Twitter, July 4, 2019. https://bit.ly/2KsAjWl

Paschal, Olivia, and Madeleine Carlisle. "Read Ta-Nehisi Coates's Testimony on Reparations." *The Atlantic*, July 19, 2019. https://bit.ly/3elWaXQ

Peterson, Kevin C. "What July Fourth Meant to Frederick Douglass." WBUR, July 3, 2017. https://wbur.fm/3eDbGUU

Walsh, Jim. "'What to the Slave Is the Fourth of July?': Why Frederick Douglass 1852 speech still resonates." *MinnPost*, July 3, 2019. https://bit.ly/2ytqSU2

LEARNING MORE

BOOKS

Bolden, Tonya. *Facing Frederick: The Life of Frederick Douglass, a Monumental American Man*. New York: Harry N. Abrams, 2018.

Carlson-Berne, Emma. *Face of Freedom: How the Photos of Frederick Douglass Celebrated Racial Equality*. North Mankato: Capstone, 2017.

Gregory, Josh. *Frederick Douglass*. New York: Scholastic, 2015.

Prince, April Jones. *Who Was Frederick Douglass?* New York: Grosset & Dunlap, 2014.

WEBSITES

Discover more about Frederick Douglass's life: **www.frederick-douglass-heritage.org**

Learn about Cedar Hill, the historic house and visitor center dedicated to Frederick Douglass: **www.nps.gov/frdo/index.htm**

Read about the history of Juneteenth celebrations: **www.juneteenth.com**

Find out more about primary and secondary sources: **www.lib.uci.edu/introduction-primary-sources**

GLOSSARY

abolitionist A person who supported and worked for the legal ending of slavery
address A speech written or directed to a specific group of people
American Civil War A war between the northern and southern American states, which lasted from 1861–1865
American Revolution The war of 1775–1783 in which 13 British colonies in North America broke free from British rule and became the United States of America
analogy A similarity between two things from which a comparison is made
argument A discussion or debate involving different points of view
bias An opinion in favor of or against a person, group, or thing, usually in an unfair way
biographer A writer of a biography, or the story of someone's life
civilization A type of society or culture that existed in a specific time or place
class A division of people that is based on social or economic privilege or lack of it
colonists People from one country who build a settlement in another territory or land
Confederate A supporter of the Confederate States of America, which included southern states that withdrew from the U.S. in 1861
debate A discussion in a public setting where two sides put forward arguments for or against an idea
era A period of time marked by specific events
founding fathers A group of American leaders who united the Thirteen Colonies in a war of independence against Great Britain
hyperbole Obvious and intentional exaggeration
integration A system in which different groups or races are brought together
intended Designed or meant for a particular reason or purpose
legacy A lasting result of a past event
liberty Freedom from arbitrary or unlimited control or rule
metaphor A figure of speech in which a term or phrase is used to represent something else
nuanced Having subtle or slight differences or variations
patriot A person who has and shows great love and support for one's country
personification Giving human qualities to an animal, object, or idea
persuasion Convincing or urging someone to do something by appealing to reason
persuasive Intended to persuade
rebellion Working against authority, control, or the way things are usually done
reparations Making amends for a wrong that has been done through payments of money or otherwise helping those who have been wronged
simile A figure of speech in which two things that are not alike are compared
social justice The idea of just or fair treatment of relations between different members of society, governments, and institutions
Union army The army of the United States of America during the U.S. Civil War

INDEX

ABOUT THE AUTHOR

Rebecca Sjonger is the author of over 50 non-fiction books for young people. American history is one of her favorite subjects to write about. She loves the challenge of separating facts from fiction while researching.